Houghton Mifflin

Math Expressions

Volume 1

Homework and Remembering

Developed by
The Children's Math Worlds
Research Project

PROJECT DIRECTOR AND AUTHOR

Dr. Karen C. Fuson

This material is based upon work supported by the
National Science Foundation
under Grant Numbers
ESI-9816320, REC-9806020, and RED-935373.

Any opinions, findings, and conclusions or recommendations expressed in this
material are those of the author and do not necessarily reflect the views of the
National Science Foundation.

HOUGHTON MIFFLIN   BOSTON

Teacher Reviewers

Kindergarten
Patricia Stroh Sugiyama
Wilmette, Illinois

Barbara Wahle
Evanston, Illinois

Grade 1
Sandra Budson
Newton, Massachusetts

Janet Pecci
Chicago, Illinois

Megan Rees
Chicago, Illinois

Grade 2
Molly Dunn
Danvers, Massachusetts

Agnes Lesnick
Hillside, Illinois

Rita Soto
Chicago, Illinois

Grade 3
Jane Curran
Honesdale, Pennsylvania

Sandra Tucker
Chicago, Illinois

Grade 4
Sara Stoneberg Llibre
Chicago, Illinois

Sheri Roedel
Chicago, Illinois

Grade 5
Todd Atler
Chicago, Illinois

Leah Barry
Norfolk, Massachusetts

Credits

Cover art: (puppy) © Frank Siteman/age fotostock. (kitten) © Photodisc/Getty Images.
(blocks) © HMCo./Richard Hutchings.

Illustrative art: Ginna Magee and Burgandy Beam/Wilkinson Studio; Tim Johnson
Technical art: Anthology, Inc.

Printed in the U.S.A.

ISBN-13: 978-0-618-64106-2
ISBN-10: 0-618-64106-8

3 4 5 6 7 8 9   EB 11 10 09 08 07

1-11

Name

Homework

Draw 5 trees.	Draw 3 bees.
Draw 4 rocks.	Draw 2 socks.

On the Back Draw 3 people. Then practice writing the numbers 1 and 2.

UNIT 1 LESSON 11

Count From 1–10 1

2

2 2 2 2 2 2 2

2

Name _____

Homework

Ring the pictures that are the same/alike.

Cross out the picture that is different/not alike.

1.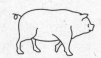

6.

2.

7.

3.

8.

4.

9.

5.

10.

On the Back Draw 2 birds that are the same size and 1 bird that is a different size. Then practice writing the number 3.

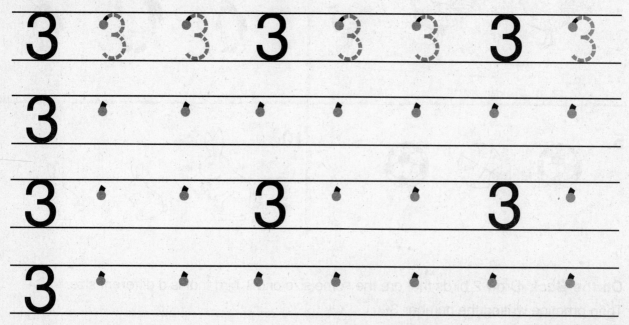

Exploration of Shapes

Name _____

Practice

Ring the pictures that are the same/alike.

Cross out the picture that is different/not alike.

1.

2.

3.

4.

5.

6.

7.

8.

9.

10.

On the Back Draw a picture of 3 things that are different. Then practice writing the number 3.

Objects and Numbers Through 10: Square-Inch Tiles **5**

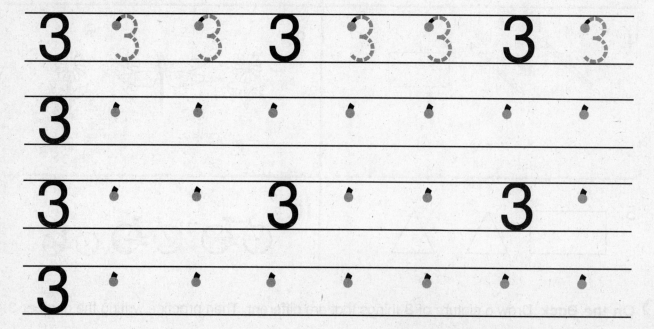

Objects and Numbers Through 10: Square-Inch Tiles

Homework

Name _____

Draw 2 dogs.	Draw 4 logs.
Draw 3 bugs.	Draw 5 mugs.

On the Back Draw 5 animals. Then practice writing the numbers 1 and 2.

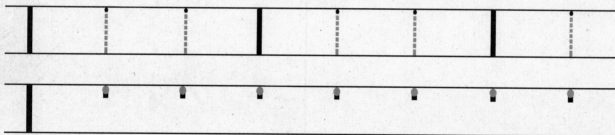

Number of Objects in a Group

Practice

Go left to right. Ring groups of the number. X out groups that are not the number.

3

4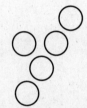

5

2

➡ **On the Back** Draw a group of 5 squares. Then practice writing the number 3.

2- and 3-Dimensional Shapes: Circle and Ball **9**

Name _____

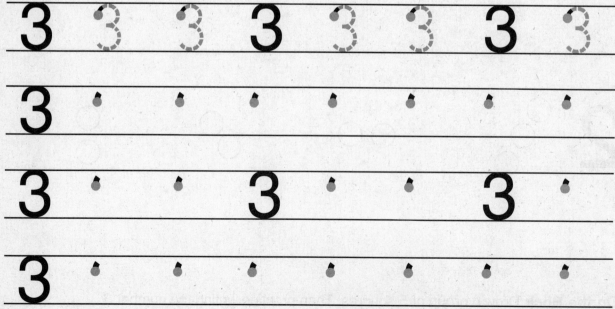

2- and 3-Dimensional Shapes: Circle and Ball

Homework

Draw 5 eggs.	Draw 2 legs.
Draw 4 boats.	Draw 3 coats.

➡ **On the Back** Draw 2 goats. Then practice writing the number 4.

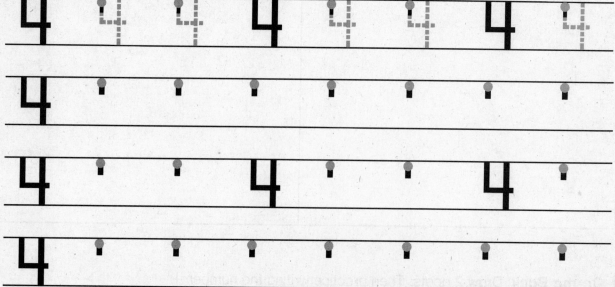

More Numbers of Objects in a Group

Name _____

Practice

Go left to right. Ring groups of the number. X out groups that are not the number.

3

4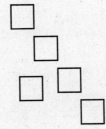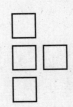

5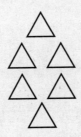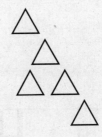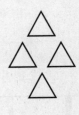

2

🔵 **On the Back** Draw 4 triangles. Then practice writing the number 4.

Objects and Numbers Through 10: Centimeter Cubes **13**

Name _____

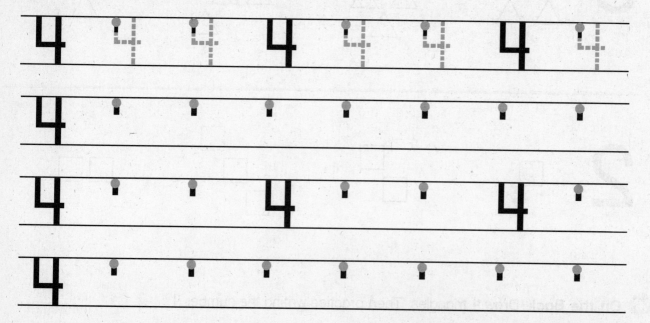

Objects and Numbers Through 10: Centimeter Cubes

Name _____

Homework

Go left to right. Ring groups of the number. X out groups that are not the number.

3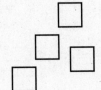

4

5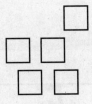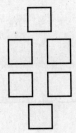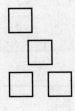

2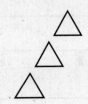

On the Back Draw a group of 5 cherries. Then practice writing the number 5.

Practice: Number of Objects in a Group **15**

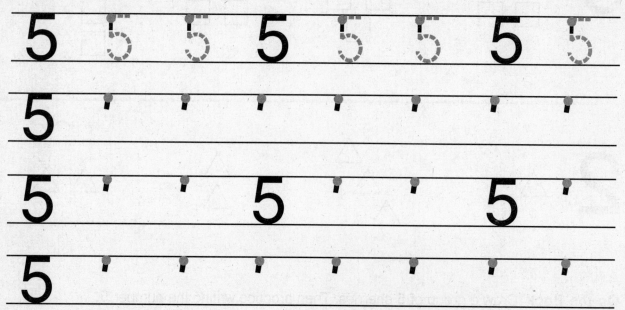

Practice: Number of Objects in a Group

Homework

Connect the dots in order.

•1 •3 •2	•2 •4 •1 •3
•2 •1 •3 •4	•1 •3 •5 •2 •4

On the Back Practice drawing straight lines. Draw lines that go up and down. Also draw lines that go from left to right.

More Objects and Numbers Through 10: Square-Inch Tiles

Homework

Name _____

Go left to right. Ring groups of the number. X out groups that are not the number.

3

4

5

2

On the Back Draw a group of 2 and a group of 4. Then practice writing the number 5.

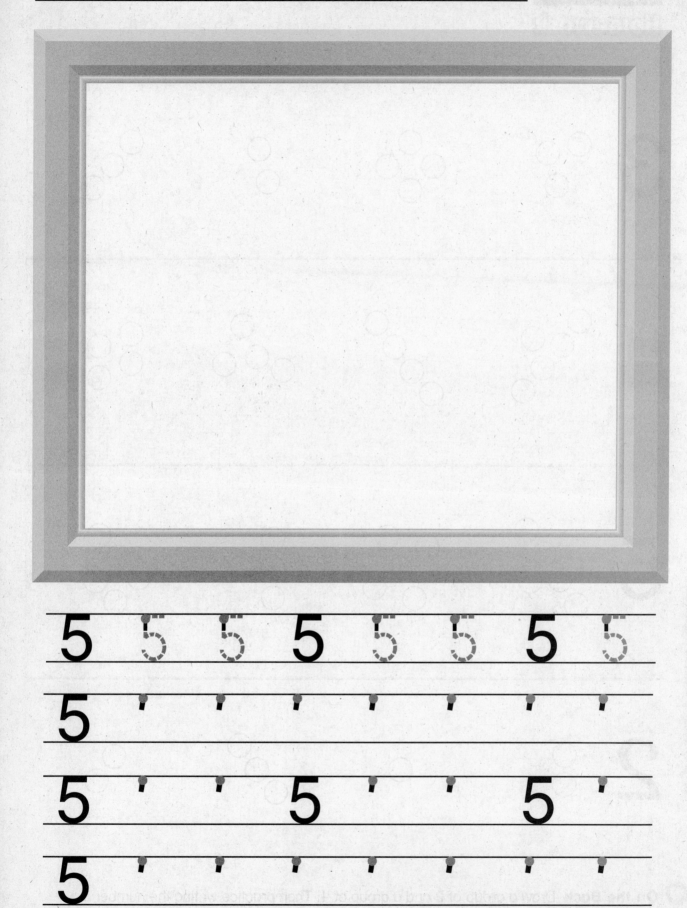

5 5 5 5 5 5 5

5

5 5 5

5

More Scenes of 2, 3, 4, and 5

Practice

Name _____

---

1. Draw 5 bugs.

2. Draw 2 rugs.

3. Draw 4 trucks.

4. Draw 3 ducks.

➡ **On the Back** Practice writing the numbers 1, 2, 3, 4, and 5.

More Objects and Numbers Through 10: Centimeter Cubes **21**

Name _____

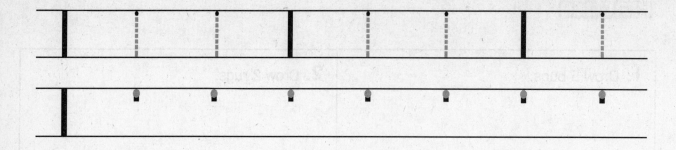

1

1

2 2 2 2 2 2 2 2

2

3 3 3 3 3 3 3 3

3

4 4 4 4 4 4 4 4

4

5 5 5 5 5 5 5 5

5

More Objects and Numbers Through 10: Centimeter Cubes

Name _____

Homework

Go left to right. Ring groups of the number. X out groups that are not the number.

3

4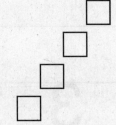

5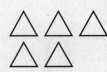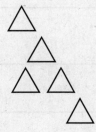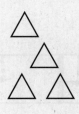

2

➡ **On the Back** Practice writing the numbers 1, 2, 3, 4, and 5.

1 1 1 1 1 1 1

1

2 2 2 2 2 2 2 2

2

3 3 3 3 3 3 3 3

3

4 4 4 4 4 4 4 4

4

5 5 5 5 5 5 5 5

5

Scenes of I

Name _____

Practice

Connect the dots in order.

2   4

· 2   · 4

1   3   5

· 1   · 3   · 5

1
· 1

2
· 2

3
· 3

4
· 4

5
· 5

1   2

· 1   · 2

3
· 3

4   5

· 4   · 5

1   3   5

· 1   · 3   · 5

2   4

· 2   · 4

On the Back Draw your own dot-to-dot picture.

Name _____

Make a Class Graph

Homework

Name _____

Go left to right. Ring groups of the number. X out groups that are not the number.

2

5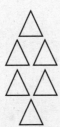

4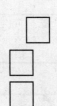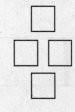

3

On the Back Draw a group of 6. Then practice writing the numbers 1, 2, 3, 4, and 5.

Name _____

Homework

Ring groups of the number. X out groups that are not the number.

6

7

8

9

10

  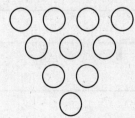 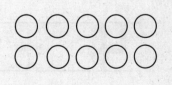

 On the Back Draw a group of 8. Then practice writing the numbers 1, 2, 3, 4, and 5.

1

2

3

4

5

Family Math Stories

Name _____

Homework

Ring groups of the number. X out groups that are not the number.

6

7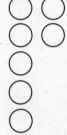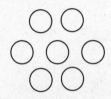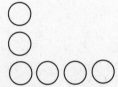

8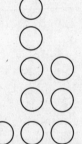

9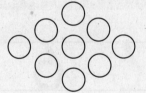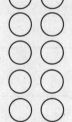

10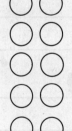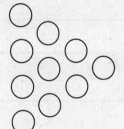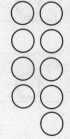

➡ **On the Back** Draw a group of 6. Then practice writing the number 6.

More Family Math Stories

Name _____

Ring groups of the number. X out groups that are not the number.

6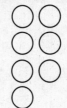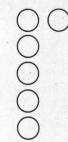

7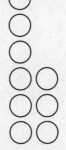

8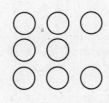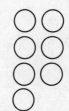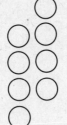

9

10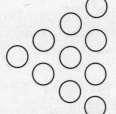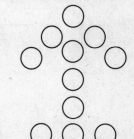

➡ **On the Back** Draw 8 circles. Use a 5-group.

Make Repeating Patterns

Practice

Continue the pattern.

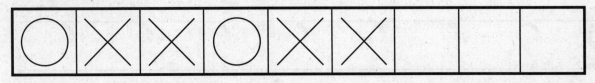

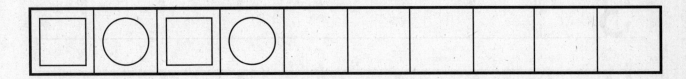

| 2 | 3 | 2 | 3 | | | | | |

| C | C | D | C | C | D | | | |

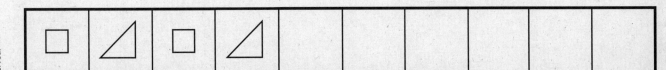

Draw your own patterns.

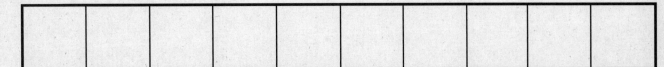

⬅ **On the Back** Practice writing the numbers 1–6.

1

2 2

3 3

4 4

5 5

6 6

Addition and Subtraction Stories: Playground Scenario

Homework

Name _____

Connect the dots in order.

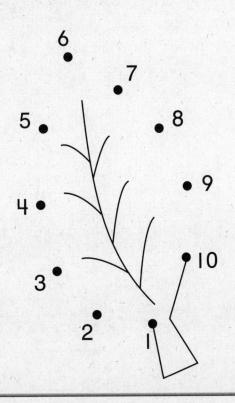

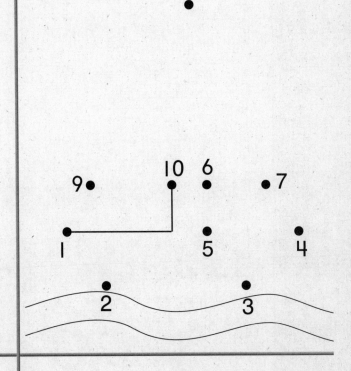

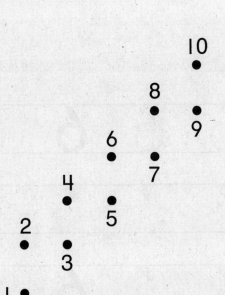

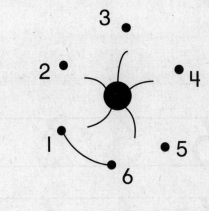

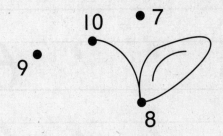

⬤ **On the Back** Draw 6 flowers. Then practice writing the number 6.

More Coin Values and Numbers 6–10 **37**

6 6 6 6 6 6 6

6

6 6 6

6

Name _____

Practice

Ring groups of the number. X out groups that are not the number.

6

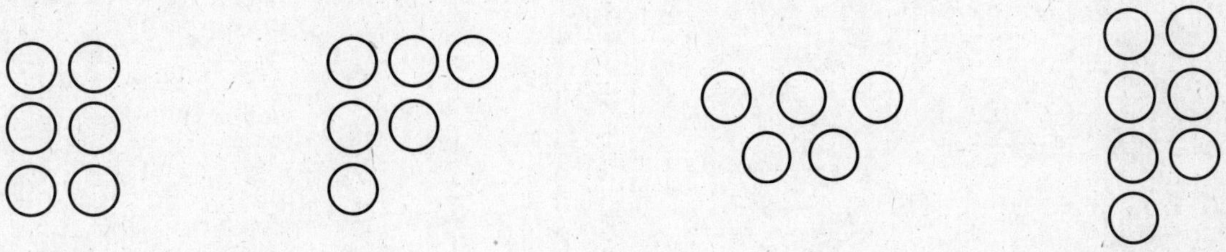

7

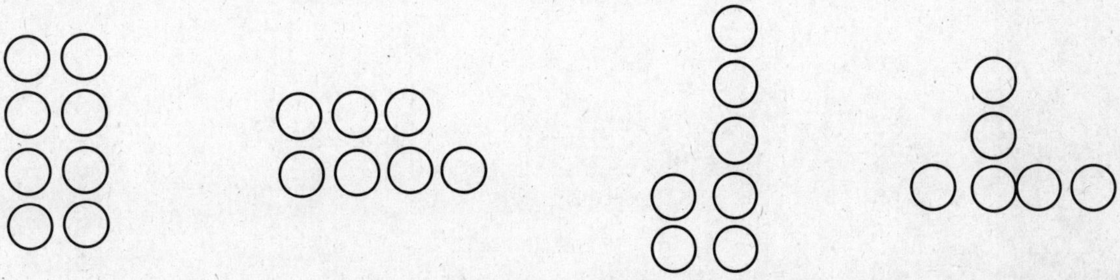

8

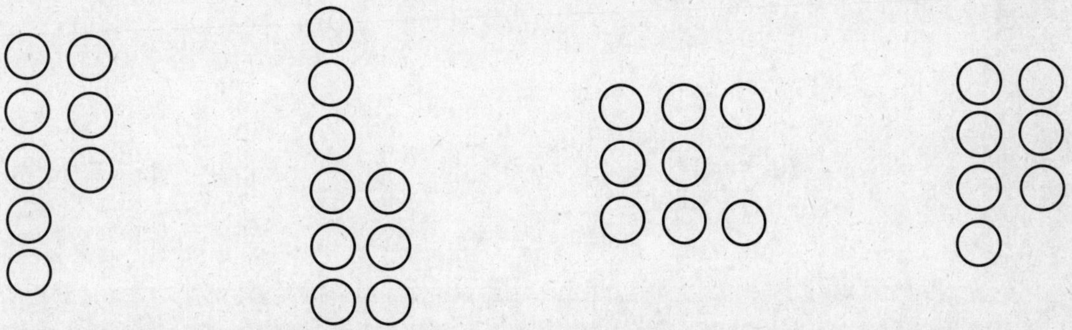

9

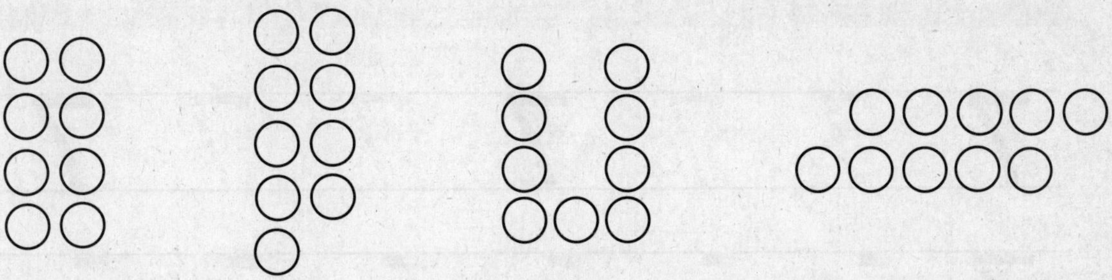

10

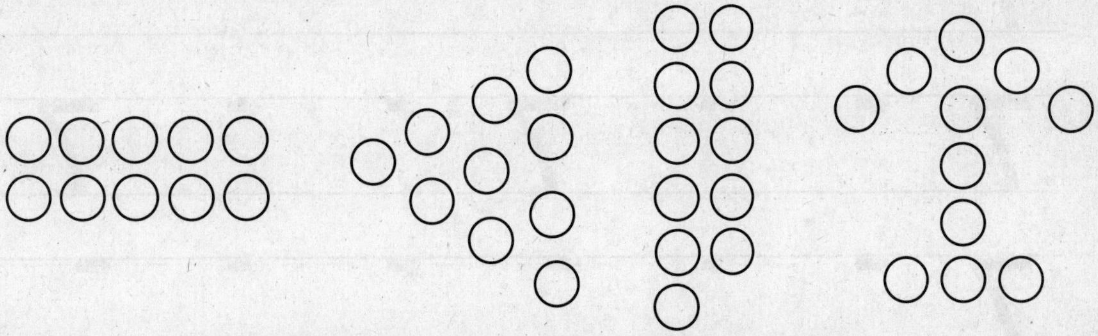

➡ **On the Back** Draw a group of 7 rectangles. Then practice writing the number 7.

2- and 3-Dimensional Shapes: Rectangles and Boxes **39**

Name _____

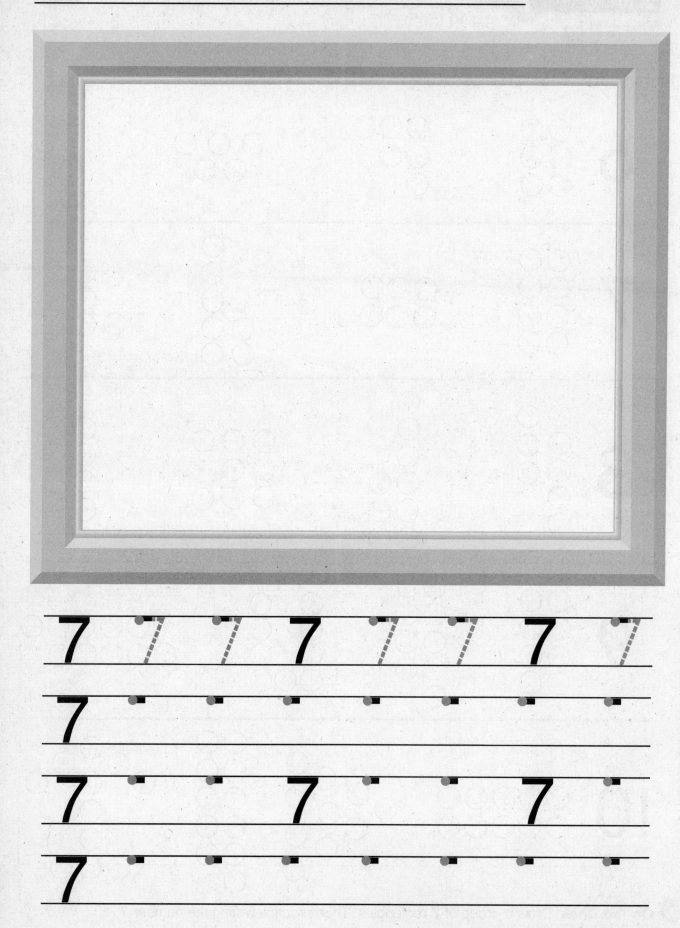

2- and 3-Dimensional Shapes: Rectangles and Boxes

Homework

Draw shapes in each box to show that number.

1	2
3	4
5	

➡ **On the Back** Use shapes to draw patterns.

Name

Practice with 5-Groups

Ring groups of the number. X out groups that are not the number.

6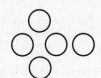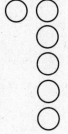

7

8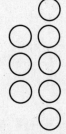

9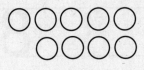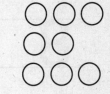

10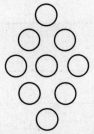

🡒 **On the Back** Draw 8 bugs. Then practice writing the number 8.

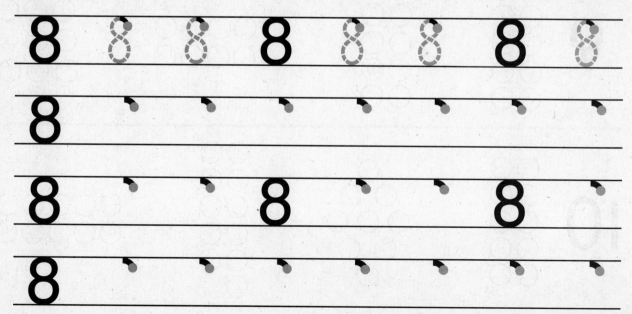

Explore Number Patterns

Practice

Name _____

Ring groups of the number. X out groups that are not the number.

6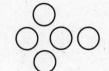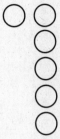

7

8

9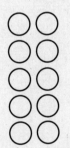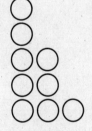

10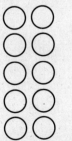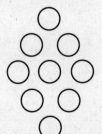

➡ **On the Back** Draw a group of 9 rectangles.

Name

More Repeating Patterns

Homework

Name _____

Use a pencil or marker and trace
each number 2 times.

| 3 | ● ● ● |
| 5 | ● ● ● ● ● |

3 5   5   3
   3   3   3   5   3
5
     5   3   5   5
5   3   3   5   5
                           3
3   5   5   5   3   5   3
         5   3   3   3   5
5   3   3   5

Write numbers 1–10.

➡ **On the Back** Draw 5 triangles. Write the number 5.

Relate Shapes and Numbers 6–10

Practice

Name _____

Use a pencil or marker and trace
each number 2 times.

4	● ● ● ●

6	● ● ● ● ●

6 4 6 4
4 6 6
4 6
6 6 4 6
4 4 6
4 6
6 4 6
4 4 6 6

Write numbers 1–8.

➡ **On the Back** Draw 9 carrots. Then practice writing the number 9.

Copyright © Houghton Mifflin Company. All rights reserved.

UNIT 2 LESSON 16

Addition and Subtraction Stories: Garden Scenario **49**

Name _____

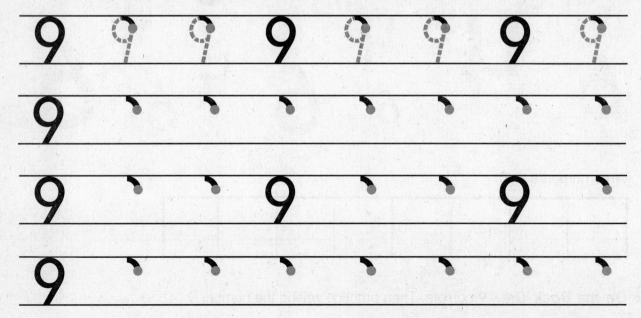

Addition and Subtraction Stories: Garden Scenario

Draw 6 hats.

Draw 9 mats.

Draw 7 cats.

Draw 8 bats.

 On the Back Write the numbers 1–9 in all different sizes.

Numbers I Through 10: the +I Pattern

Name _____

Homework

Continue the pattern.

2	5	2	5						

◯	▭	◯	▭						

☐	◯	◯	☐	◯	◯			

△	△	△	△	△	△			

3	3	5	3	3	5			

Draw your own patterns.

➡ **On the Back** Draw your own patterns.

More Numbers 1 Through 10: the +1 Pattern

Practice

Name _____

Use a pencil or marker and trace
each number 2 times.

| 4 | ● ● ● ● |

| 8 | ● ● ● ● ●
● ● ● ● |

8
4
8
8
4
4
4
8
4
8
8
4
4
8
8
8
4
4
8
4
8
4
8
4
8
4
8
8
4
4
8
8

Write the numbers 1–10.

➡ **On the Back** Draw a picture of 4 children playing.

Addition and Subtraction Stories: Family Experience **55**

Name _____

Addition and Subtraction Stories: Family Experience

Homewor

Name _____

Draw 7 cars.	Draw 6 jars.

Draw 9 books.	Draw 8 hooks.

On the Back Draw a group of 10. Then practice writing the number 10.

Name _____

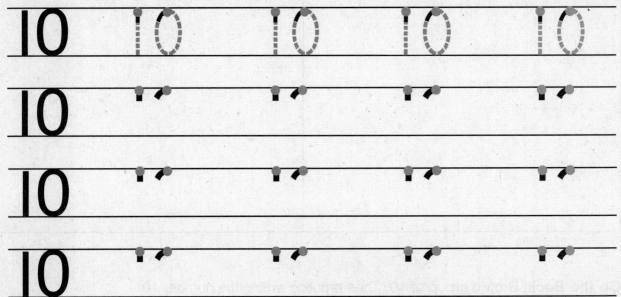

10 10 10 10 10

10 10 10 10 10

10 10 10 10 10

10 10 10 10 10

Numbers 1 Through 10: the −1 Pattern

Name _____

Practice

Use a pencil or marker and trace
each number 2 times.

| 5 | ● ● ● ● ● |

| 9 | ● ● ● ● ● |
| | ● ● ● ● |

9 9 9
5   5   5
9   5   9   5
9   5   9
9   5
5   9   5   9   5
9   5
5   9   5   9
9   5
9   9   5   9   5   9

Write the numbers 1–10.

➡ **On the Back** Write the numbers 1–9 in all different sizes.

Homework

Write numbers 4 and 5.

Draw 4 things.	Draw 4 rectangles.

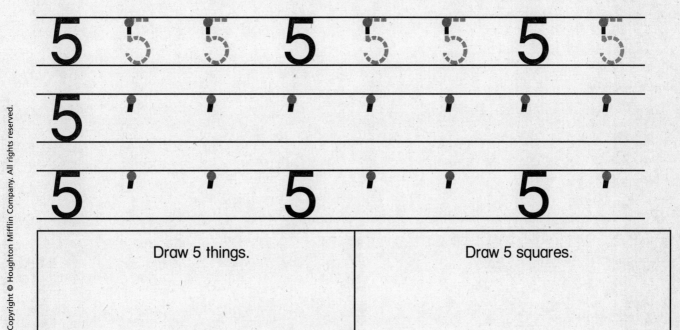

Draw 5 things.	Draw 5 squares.

 On the Back Draw 10 animals.

More Numbers 1 Through 10: the −1 Pattern

Homework

Name _____

Use a pencil or marker. Trace all the
numbers 2 times.

| 3 | ● ● ● |
| 8 | ● ● ● ● ● ● ● ● |

8 8
3 8
3
3 8
3 8 3
8
8 8 3 3 8
3 8
3
3 3
3 8
3 8 8 3
3 8 8 8
8

Write numbers 1–10.

➡ **On the Back** Write the number 8, and draw 8 trees.

Groups of 10 **63**

Name _____

Homework

I. Finish the 5-group that shows the same number.

 = ☐

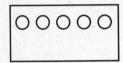

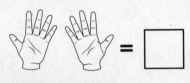 = ☐

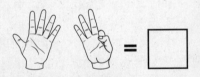 = ☐

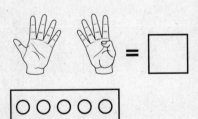 = ☐

2. Finish the 5-groups.

7 = ⬭⬭⬭⬭⬭

9 = ⬭⬭⬭⬭⬭

6 = ⬭⬭⬭⬭⬭

8 = ⬭⬭⬭⬭⬭

8 = ⬭⬭⬭⬭⬭

10 = ⬭⬭⬭⬭⬭

10 = ⬭⬭⬭⬭⬭

6 = ⬭⬭⬭⬭⬭

3. Write the number.

⬭⬭⬭⬭⬭ / ⬭⬭ = ☐   ⬭⬭⬭⬭⬭ / ⬭⬭⬭⬭ = ☐

⬭⬭⬭⬭⬭ / ⬭⬭⬭⬭⬭ = ☐   ⬭⬭⬭ = ☐

⬭⬭⬭⬭⬭ / ⬭⬭⬭ = ☐   ⬭⬭⬭⬭⬭ / ⬭⬭⬭ = ☐

⬭⬭⬭⬭⬭ / ⬭ = ☐   ⬭⬭⬭⬭⬭ = ☐

➡ **On the Back** Draw 2 hands that show the number 10.

Practice Addition and Subtraction Stories: Park Scenario

Homework

Name _____

1. Write the number pattern in each row.

••	•••••	••••• •••	••	•••••	••••• •••	••	•••••	••••• •••
2	5	8	2	5	8	2	5	8

2. Repeat the pattern.

▶ **On the Back** Write the numbers 1–20.

More Attributes: Size, Shape, and Color **73**

1	11		1	11		
2	12					
3	13					
4	14					
5	15					
6	16					
7	17					
8	18					
9	19					
10	20		10	20		

More Attributes: Size, Shape, and Color

Name _____

Practice

1. Continue the pattern.

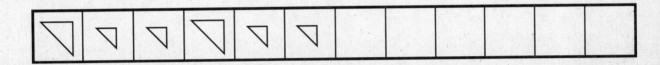

| 7 | 8 | 7 | 8 | | | | | | | | |

| L | M | N | L | M | N | | | | | | |

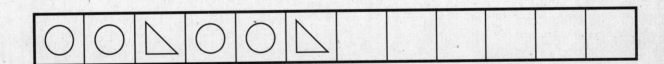

| 6 | 6 | 8 | 6 | 6 | 8 | | | | | | |

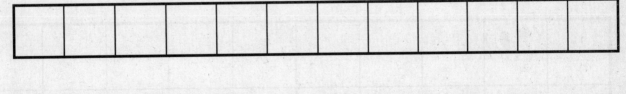

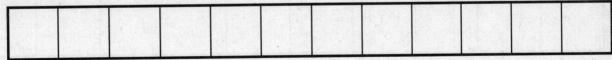

2. Draw your own patterns.

| | | | | | | | | | | | |

| | | | | | | | | | | | |

➡ **On the Back** Draw 9 different flowers. Then write the numbers 1–20.

Build Teen Numbers with Square-Inch Tiles **75**

Name

Build Teen Numbers with Square-Inch Tiles

Name _____

Homework

1. Draw circles for 1–10.
Show the 5-groups.

1	
2	
3	
4	
5	
6	
7	○ ○ ○ ○ ○ ○ ○
8	
9	
10	

2. Finish the 5-groups.

6 = ○ ○ ○ ○ ○   8 = ○ ○ ○ ○ ○

8 = ○ ○ ○ ○ ○   9 = ○ ○ ○ ○ ○

10 = ○ ○ ○ ○ ○   7 = ○ ○ ○ ○ ○

9 = ○ ○ ○ ○ ○   10 = ○ ○ ○ ○ ○

3. Write the number.

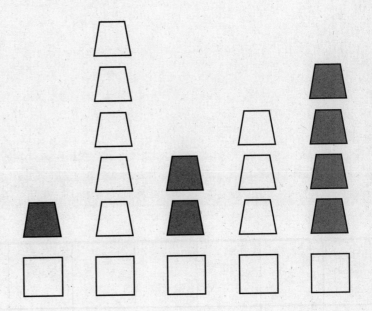

4. On the Back Draw 7 different houses. Then write the numbers 1–20.

Attribute Card Activities **77**

Name _____

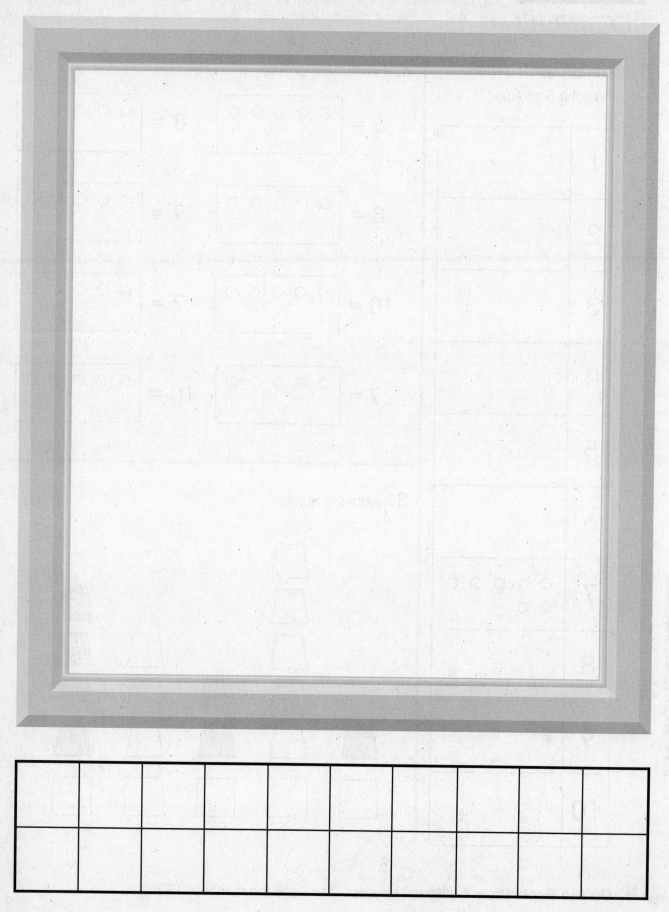

Attribute Card Activities

Name _____

Practice

Write the number.

1.

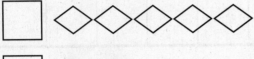

2.

3.

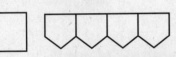

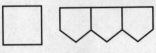

4.

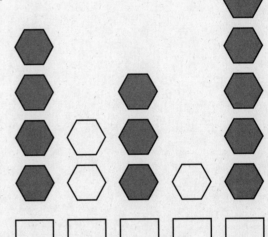

Finish the pattern.

5.

8	8	2	8	8	2						

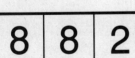

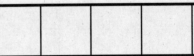

⟶ **On the Back** Draw your own patterns.

Partners of Teen Numbers

Homework

1. Write the number pattern in each row.

4	6	9	4	6	9	4	6	9

2. Repeat the pattern.

On the Back Write the numbers 1–10 in all d____nt sizes.

2- and 3-Dimensional Shapes: Squares and Cubes **83**

Name

2- and 3-Dimensional Shapes: Squares and Cubes

Homework

Name _____

Write the partners.

2

☐ + ☐

3

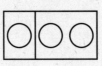

☐ + ☐

3

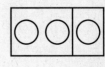

☐ + ☐

4

☐ + ☐

4

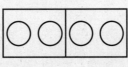

☐ + ☐

4

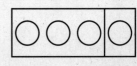

☐ + ☐

5

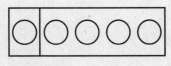

☐ + ☐

5

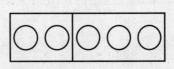

☐ + ☐

5

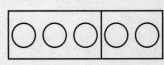
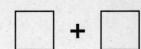

☐ + ☐

6

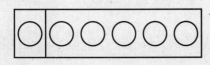

☐ + ☐

6

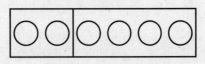

☐ + ☐

6

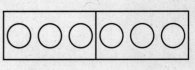

☐ + ☐

On the Back Draw a picture for 2 + 3 in the top box.

Draw a picture for 3 + 1 in the bottom box.

More Graph Drawings: Match and Compare **85**

Name _____

More Graph Drawings: Match and Compare

Name _____

Practice

Write the number pattern in each row.

●●●	●●●●	●●●●●	●●●	●●●●	●●●●●	●●●	●●●●	●●●●●
3	4	5	3	4	5	3	4	5

Repeat the pattern.

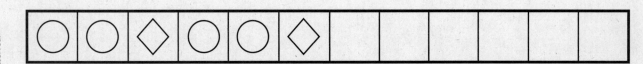

| ▽ | △ | ▽ | △ | | | | | | |

| ○ | ○ | ◇ | ○ | ○ | ◇ | | | | | |

| J | K | L | J | K | L | | | | | |

🢂 **On the Back** Draw your own patterns.

Name

More Teen Numbers with Classroom Objects

Name _____

Homework

Draw circles for 1–10. Show the 5-groups.

1	
2	
3	
4	
5	
6	
7	
8	
9	○ ○ ○ ○ ○ ○ ○ ○ ○
10	

Write each number and = or ≠.

$\boxed{2}$ ≠ $\boxed{4}$

$\square$ $\square$

$\square$ $\square$ $\square$ $\square$

$\square$ $\square$ $\square$ $\square$

$\square$ $\square$ $\square$ $\square$

Finish the 5-groups.

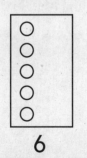
6

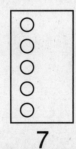
7

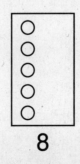
8

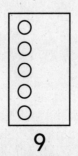
9

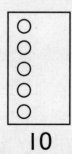
10

On the Back Draw two groups of circles. Write = or ≠.

More Attribute Card Activities **89**

More Attribute Card Activities

Name

Practice

1. Finish the 5-group to show the number.

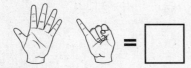 = ☐

○ ○ ○ ○ ○

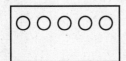 = ☐

○ ○ ○ ○ ○

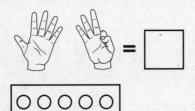 = ☐

○ ○ ○ ○ ○

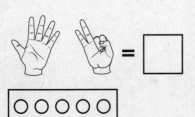 = ☐

○ ○ ○ ○ ○

2. Finish the 5-groups.

10 = ○○○○○   8 = ○○○○○

6 = ○○○○○   6 = ○○○○○

7 = ○○○○○   8 = ○○○○○

9 = ○○○○○   7 = ○○○○○

3. Write the number.

○○○○ / ○○○ = ☐   ○○ = ☐

○○○○○ / ○ = ☐   ○○○○○ / ○○ = ☐

○○○○○ / ○○ = ☐   ○○○○○ / ○ = ☐

○○○○○ / ○○○○ = ☐   ○○○○○ = ☐

On the Back Use shapes to make a picture.

Name _____

Object Collections: Teen Numbers

Homework

Write the number pattern in each row.

◆◆◆	◆◆◆◆◆ ◆	◆◆◆◆◆ ◆◆◆◆	◆◆◆	◆◆◆◆◆ ◆	◆◆◆◆◆ ◆◆◆◆	◆◆◆	◆◆◆◆◆ ◆	◆◆◆◆◆ ◆◆◆◆
3	6	9	3	6	9	3	6	9

Write each number and = or ≠.

| 5 | = | 5 |

 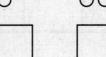

On the Back Write the numbers 1–20.

1	2	3	4	5	6	7	8	9	10
11	12	13	14	15	16	17	18	19	20

1									10
11									20

Shapes in a Garden Scene